Spiritual Independence

An Introduction to Soka Spirit

Prepared by the SGI-USA Soka Spirit Committee

Published by SGI-USA

606 Wilshire Blvd., Santa Monica CA 90401

www.sgi-usa.org

Cover photo © Evelyn McGeever/iStockphoto

Design by Stephanie Sydney/syd.art, Inc.

ISBN 978-1-932911-80-0

Table of Contents

Editor's Note

There are two paramount beliefs embraced in Nichiren Buddhism: 1) the absolute sanctity of human life; and 2) opposition to forces that diminish human life. These beliefs are what inform the actions of the SGI in relation to the Nichiren Shoshu priesthood. To value one life over another is anathema to Nichiren's teachings.

The short essays in this pamphlet briefly explain the principles and behaviors pertaining to the Nichiren Shoshu priesthood's deviation from Nichiren Buddhism and its attempt to disband the Soka Gakkai International and distort the Buddhist view of good and evil.

A speech by SGI President Ikeda explains the events surrounding the separation of the priesthood and laity in light of the teachings of Nichiren Daishonin.

The challenge to practice exactly as Nichiren Daishonin intended and as demonstrated by the three founding presidents of the Soka Gakkai is called Soka Spirit.

The citations most commonly used in this publication have been abbreviated as follows:

WND-1 and WND-2 refer to *The Writings of Nichiren Daishonin*, volumes 1 and 2 respectively (Tokyo: Soka Gakkai, 1999 [vol. 1] and 2006 [vol. 2]).

Introduction
The Struggle Against Delusion

What would cause the relatively small Nichiren Shoshu clergy of a few thousand priests to call for the dissolution of the Soka Gakkai International lay organization of more than 10 million members? Why would a clergy with a negligible presence outside Japan cut itself off from a laity that is growing in more than 190 countries? Why would priests corrupt the very teachings they were meant to protect?

> ## Key Points
> ■ The history of the Soka Gakkai International, dedicated to the achievement of world peace, attests to the validity of encountering opposition as the foremost proponent of the sutra's principles embodied in Nichiren Buddhism, just as foretold in the Lotus Sutra.

One answer might be the influence of what sociology calls "institutionalization." It means that once a bureaucracy of ritual and formality is created — in this case, around Nichiren Buddhism — "There is the possibility of substantial deviation in values," according to sociologist B. Guy Peters.

When a bureaucratic infrastructure grows up around a religion, powerful forces within human nature come into play that can work against the original intent of the founder's teaching. Ultimately, the power, prosperity and survival of the infrastructure can take priority over the very teaching it was supposed to protect and propagate. This can lead to adapting or distorting the teachings to support the continued existence of the religious bureaucracy and those in authority. But there is a deeper view of the priesthood's opposition to the SGI found in Buddhist scripture.

The Lotus Sutra tells us that those propagating its revolutionary teachings will encounter opposition because, "This Lotus Sutra is the most difficult to believe and the most difficult to understand" (*The Lotus Sutra*, p. 164). One reason for this difficulty is its revelation that all people without exception are fundamentally worthy of respect because they possess the Buddha nature. Another reason is that it provides the foundation for a people-centered religion, something unprecedented in history. The history of the Soka Gakkai International attests to the validity of encountering opposition as the foremost proponent of the sutra's principles embodied in Nichiren Buddhism.

When the Soka Gakkai was founded in 1930 by first and second presidents Tsunesaburo Makiguchi and Josei Toda, they embraced the lineage of the Fuji school founded by Nichiren's successor, Nikko, and represented by Nichiren Shoshu, a small and impoverished school of Nichiren Buddhism. For the next sixty years, the progressive lay movement of the Soka Gakkai struggled to maintain a harmonious relationship with an anachronistic, fundamentalist priesthood. From the beginning, it was clear that the two had conflicting priorities. The priests of Nichiren Shoshu, with a nearly 700-year history, were focused on maintaining their order. The Soka Gakkai, inspired by its founders, was focused on Nichiren's mandate to accomplish *kosen-rufu*, the widespread propagation of his teachings.

It was President Makiguchi who first proposed the creation of a format for reciting the Lotus Sutra as part of the daily practice of lay believers. The appearance of a proactive laity that embraced the mission to accomplish *kosen-rufu* was a huge departure from the approach of previous followers of the Nichiren Shoshu priesthood.

By the 1970s and '80s, Nichiren Shoshu had become very wealthy through the support of the Soka Gakkai lay believers. Eventually, it became clear to the priesthood that the self-empowering practice of Nichiren Buddhism precluded the laity and its resources ever being controlled by priests, and they made a desperate attempt to seize control.

In November 1991, the Nichiren Shoshu priesthood, under the leadership of its high priest, Nikken Abe, excommunicated all of the more than 10 million SGI members. Their hope was to pull a large percentage of Soka Gakkai members into their temples. That didn't happen.

On one level, the crux of the conflict was the clergy's insistence that priests are necessary intermediaries between lay believers and the power and teachings of Nichiren Buddhism. Emphasizing ritual

and formality not found in Nichiren Daishonin's teachings, the priests sought to make veneration and obedience to themselves and their high priest in particular the most important aspect of a practitioner's faith.

They stressed, for example, that funeral services must be officiated by priests in order for the deceased to become enlightened, and they demanded exorbitant donations from ordinary believers for those simple services. They upheld the view that, without venerating the high priest, practitioners could not attain enlightenment.

Nichiren Daishonin clearly denounced such views in his writings, emphasizing the empowerment of ordinary believers to attain enlightenment.

"Never seek this Gohonzon [Buddhahood] outside yourself," Nichiren instructs a lay believer. "The Gohonzon exists only within the mortal flesh of us ordinary people who embrace the Lotus Sutra and chant Nam-myoho-renge-kyo" (WND-1, 832).

The priesthood claimed that faith was infused with power and validated only through the authority of the high priest. The SGI stressed a faith based on the inherent power of the individual. This is the difference between dependency and self-reliance, between deference and empowerment.

> ■ The priesthood claims that faith is validated only through the high priest. The SGI stresses faith based on the inherent power of the individual. This is the difference between dependency and self-reliance, between deference and empowerment.

James Thew/iStockphoto

All people are equally endowed with the power of the Law.

On another level, this issue originates in the spiritual struggle between opposing forces within the human heart. SGI President Ikeda states: "Chanting in terms of faith refers to the spiritual aspect of our practice. This essentially consists of the struggle we wage in our hearts against our inner delusion or darkness — a battle against the negative and destructive forces within us. It means that through the power of faith — in other words, through strengthening our conviction that we possess the Buddha nature — we can break through the darkness obscuring this awareness, thus revealing the life state of Buddhahood" (September 2006 *Living Buddhism*, p. 79).

"Correct faith is grounded in the realization that 'Shakyamuni Buddha who attained enlightenment countless kalpas ago, the Lotus Sutra that leads all people to Buddhahood, and we ordinary human beings are in no way different or separate from one another' (WND-1, 216). This is a crucial point concerning the substance of faith in the Mystic Law. In this writing, Nichiren states that chanting Nam-myoho-renge-kyo with this belief is 'a matter of the utmost importance' for his disciples (WND-1, 216). The core message of this statement is to believe that our present self is an entity of Myoho-renge-kyo and that we can attain Buddhahood in our present form in this lifetime" (May–June 2008 *Living Buddhism*, p. 46). All people are equally endowed with the power of the Law — clergy and laity alike.

From the early days of the Soka Gakkai, under founding president Tsunesaburo Makiguchi and second president Josei Toda, the priesthood benefited enormously in material gain and prestige.

In spite of those gains, as the laity grew into a worldwide force of millions of believers, the priesthood continued to demonstrate numerous signs of corruption and authoritarianism.

Whenever Soka Gakkai members challenged these attitudes and irresponsible behavior by priests, calling for reform, the priesthood only became more adamant in enforcing the subordination of Soka Gakkai members. The more the Soka Gakkai grew, the more authoritarian and corrupt the priesthood became.

Finally, in 1990, after having amassed a huge financial foundation from the donations of Soka Gakkai members, Nikken formulated a plan he called "Operation C" designed to "Cut" the Soka Gakkai members off from their mentor, SGI President Ikeda, and disband the organization.

He implemented that plan by taking a series of unilateral actions against President Ikeda and the Soka Gakkai. Ultimately, Operation C sprang from Nikken's incorrect understanding and distortion of Nichiren Daishonin's teachings.

The priesthood excommunicated the entire organization in 1991, under the assumption that members would then be compelled to leave the SGI and become directly affiliated with a local temple.

The opposite occurred: The vast majority of members continued to practice within the SGI, under the leadership of President Ikeda. In short, the priesthood excommunicated itself from the body of practitioners sincerely devoted to achieving *kosen-rufu*.

In the decades since, President Ikeda has led the propagation of Nichiren Buddhism into 192 countries and territories; more than 12 million SGI members chant Nam-myoho-renge-kyo in places as diverse as the United States, Brazil, Denmark, Russia, India and South Africa.

One of the reasons the SGI is so diverse is that it refuses to tolerate structures that value one human being more than others. These can be institutional structures like the priesthood over the laity, or they can be racist structures. Separation from the priesthood was a valuable process for sensitizing SGI members to issues of structural injustice and institutional inequality.

> ■ Just pointing out the errors of the priesthood is not enough. We must eliminate both our own tendencies to be authoritarian and to be dependent on authority, overcoming disbelief in our Buddha nature and that of others.

Seikyo Press

Who controls what is holy?

This issue raises the question of who controls or administers what is holy or sacred in the universe and in the human heart. Should the essence of a religion belong exclusively to an elite class of ordained clergy?

Probably since the dawn of recorded history, it has mostly been a special group or caste of priests, shamans or monks who claimed to be divinely chosen to be the keepers of religious secrets and teachings unfathomable to common people. However, the principles of the Lotus Sutra as embodied in Nichiren Buddhism define a self-reliant, people-centered religion rather than a clergy-centered one. The Law that governs all life and phenomena in the universe is equally accessible to all people.

As mentioned earlier, the nature of religious institutions is that frequently the success and survival of the religious bureaucracy take precedence over the purity of the teachings it professes. Clerical authority will distort, change and invent new teachings to secure its authority and prosperity.

The teaching of Nichiren Buddhism, by its very nature, rejects authoritarian power. When the SGI put these self-empowering teachings into practice, the Nichiren Shoshu priesthood lost the possibility of controlling the membership and its assets and excommunicated the 10 million SGI members.

This is a matter of human rights — the rights of all people to directly access the Law, to fully embrace what is universal and sacred without intermediaries of any kind. It is a religious revolution against authoritarianism and a fundamentalist attachment to rituals and formalities.

Just pointing out the errors of the priesthood, however, is not enough. The real task is the extremely difficult transformation of the underlying cultural base that allows an authoritarian, priest-centered religion to thrive. In other words, we must eliminate both our own tendencies to be authoritarian and to be dependent on authority. It boils down to overcoming disbelief in our own Buddha nature and that of others. In his 2008 peace proposal presented to the United Nations, SGI President Ikeda writes:

"The kind of humanism I am convinced our times require is one capable of confronting and halting the slide toward fundamentalism. This is the work of restoring people and humanity to the role of central protagonist, something which ultimately can only be undertaken through a ceaseless spiritual effort to train and to temper ourselves.

"If we are to halt this slide toward fanaticism, we cannot be content to regard it as passive bystanders. A true humanist cannot avoid or abandon the struggle against evil. Humanism, as mentioned, is a word and a concept with both positive aspects — peace and tolerance, moderation — and negative possibilities — a tendency for easy compromise and merely lukewarm commitment. Unless we can break through and rise above these negative aspects, we will not be capable of countering the extremism that is the special characteristic of fanaticism" (http://sgi-usa.org/newsandevents/docs/peace2008.pdf).

Good and Evil, Devils and Enemies

"Those who call themselves my disciples and practice the Lotus Sutra should all practice as I do."

— Nichiren Daishonin (WND-1, 980)

As simple as this statement is, underlying these words is the recognition that, to practice as Nichiren did, we must surmount a powerful tendency to do the opposite; that is, to practice and believe as we are inclined to do, to be swayed by internal forces originating in the fundamental darkness of our lives.

These negative tendencies are often referred to as the "three poisons" of greed, anger and foolishness, which define a life dominated by desires, powerlessness and ignorance. They appear, and are defined, as devilish functions, evil or enemies that impede progress toward true happiness and a correct Buddhist practice as Nichiren intended.

We can observe the influence of these forces within us as selfish, egocentric thoughts and behaviors — behavior that abuses one's position and uses other people for personal gain. When we are slaves to our own arrogance and self-indulgence, we are blind to the great potential of our Buddha nature and that of others.

President Ikeda writes, "When all is said and done, faith is a struggle against self-centeredness" (*The New Human Revolution*, vol. 9, p. 143).

Key Points

■ The Lotus Sutra explains that when the Law is revealed, negative forces opposing its propagation will appear, often in the arrogant, self-centered behavior of those in power. The history of Nichiren Buddhism and the Soka Gakkai is one of overcoming efforts to hinder the propagation of Nam-myoho-renge-kyo.

iStock

Opposition appears when the Law is propagated.

The Lotus Sutra explains that when the Law is revealed, negative forces opposing its propagation will appear. These forces mostly manifest in the arrogant, self-centered behavior of those in positions of power. The history of Nichiren Buddhism and the Soka Gakkai is one of confronting and overcoming efforts to hinder the widespread propagation of the Law of Nam-myoho-renge-kyo.

Nichiren states in his writings: "The three powerful enemies will arise without fail" (WND-1, 394); "This world is the domain of the devil king of the sixth heaven " (WND-1, 495); and "As practice progresses and understanding grows, the three obstacles and four devils emerge" (WND-1, 501).

In general, these devils, enemies and obstacles represent negative functions within all people that diminish the value of life, cause disharmony, undermine our self-reliance and obstruct the progress of our Buddhist faith and practice. These are the forces of misery. These are the forces that oppose *kosen-rufu*, the propagation of the Law.

Terms like *devils*, *enemies* and *evil* represent categories of human behavior — either our own or others' — that can either aid or hinder our efforts to awaken to our inherent Buddha nature. Fortunately, if we are steadfast in faith, any obstacle, devil or enemy can become a "good friend" or positive force in our Buddhist practice, enabling our Buddha nature to emerge.

Among the negative forces known as the "three obstacles and four devils" are internal desires or doubts that can test our faith and external influences such as family or others that oppose our faith. Then there are behaviors that Buddhist scripture identifies as specifically opposing propagation of the Law. The people who behave in these ways are called the "three powerful enemies."

The oneness of good and evil is inherent in life.

Buddhism does not view good and evil or Buddha and devil as dualities. In other words, it does not teach that evil is over there and good is over here, existing independently of each other. Buddhism sees them as mutually inclusive — neither exists without the other. Where there is one, the other is an ever-present potential. Buddhism propounds the view of the "oneness of good and evil." As Nichiren explains, "Good and evil have been inherent in life since time without beginning" (WND-1, 1113).

This does not mean that good and evil are equivalent, or equally acceptable. By recognizing the potential for good within evil, we can strongly challenge injustice and wrong while striving to stimulate and nurture good. At the same time, by being aware that within good exists the potential for evil, we can always remain vigilant; we can develop the ability to recognize evil when it appears within ourselves or others, and the courage to take action to counter it.

> ■ Both fundamental enlightenment and fundamental darkness — good and evil — arise from the one Law of Nam-myoho-renge-kyo (cf. WND-1, 383). Fundamental darkness is rooted in ignorance and slander of the Law. Fundamental enlightenment is rooted in awareness of and faith in the Law.

When the terms *devil* or *evil* are applied to someone, it means that they are currently exhibiting behavior that is clearly defined as such in Buddhist teachings. But it is also understood that the opposite force is also present simultaneously. When we see good and evil in others, it means that we also see good and evil in ourselves.

Buddhism views the tension between the positive and negative energies in life as a reality of all phenomena governed by the Law of Nam-myoho-renge-kyo. Both fundamental enlightenment and fundamental darkness — good and evil — arise from the one Law of Nam-myoho-renge-kyo (cf. WND-1, 383). Fundamental darkness is rooted in ignorance and slander of the Law. Fundamental enlightenment is rooted in awareness of and faith in the Law. Either one is a force that can inform our behavior.

> When good displays its full potential by opposing evil, evil then serves a good purpose. When evil is allowed to go unchallenged, it will consume everything and all will be lost.

How we live or behave can compound our ignorance of the Law or it can lead to greater awareness of the Law. Ultimately, everything is revealed in our behavior. Nichiren states, "The purpose of the appearance in this world of Shakyamuni Buddha, the lord of teachings, lies in his behavior as a human being" (WND-1, 852). The final criteria for judging the greatness of any religion or philosophy is the behavior of those who adhere to it.

The religion or life-philosophy we embrace plays a significant role in determining which force — positive or negative — will dominate our thoughts, words and deeds, which generate life's tendencies in the form of *karma,* a Sanskrit word meaning action or behavior. A weak or incorrect philosophy of life renders us more susceptible to egocentric desires and dark urges originating from fundamental darkness or negative karma.

This tension between good and evil is especially evident in those holding positions of authority, both secular and religious, when the temptations on human nature are especially strong. This has happened repeatedly to those in positions of power among Buddhist clergy throughout history. Priests have repeatedly succumbed to baser human emotions and viewed themselves in a superior manner contrary to the very teachings they professed to follow. Their arrogance has led them to subvert the teachings entrusted to them. Nichiren himself faced this very same struggle as he explains: "The devil king of the sixth heaven has attempted to take possession of my body. But I have for some time been taking such great care that he now no longer comes near me" (WND-1, 310).

Because Nichiren defeated his own fundamental darkness, he was able to manifest his Buddha nature. It is contrary to the nature of life to expect to experience happiness without subduing our tendency to be unhappy. It is important to note that when good displays its full potential by opposing evil, evil then serves a good purpose. When evil is allowed to go unchallenged, it will consume everything and all will be lost. It is in this spirit that the SGI speaks out against the distortions of the Nichiren Shoshu priesthood.

The Story of Devadatta

The internal battle between fundamental good and fundamental evil has played out repeatedly throughout the history of Buddhism. The first and most instructive tale is the story of Devadatta. It takes place in the time of Shakyamuni Buddha in India and explains the spirit believers should adopt to protect the Buddhist Order.

Devadatta, a cousin and disciple of Shakyamuni, represents the universal tendency toward evil behavior. Driven by jealousy and ambition, he attempted to take control of the Buddhist community and lead people away from the Buddha's teachings. He lured a number of monks away from the Buddhist Order, creating a schism among the Buddha's disciples and influencing the overthrow of the king who was an ardent supporter of Shakyamuni.

Shakyamuni took immediate action to reveal the deception and severely, publicly, rebuked Devadatta.

As Nichiren explains: "The World-Honored One cursed Devadatta, saying, 'You are a fool who licks the spit of others!' Devadatta felt as though a poison arrow had been shot into his breast, and he cried out in anger, declaring: 'Gautama is no Buddha! I am the eldest son of King Dronodana, the elder brother of the Venerable Ananda, and kin to Gautama. No matter what kind of evil conduct I might be guilty

David Arky/Corbis

Key Points

■ It is by denouncing evil that we can cause such people to open their eyes. That is because hearing voices resounding with the justice of the Mystic Law has the effect of activating the Buddha nature that lies dormant in an evil person's heart.

James Thew/iStockphoto

of, he ought to admonish me in private for it. But to publicly and outrageously accuse me of faults in front of this great assembly of human and heavenly beings — is this the behavior appropriate to a great man or a Buddha?'" (WND-1, 245).

On the surface, this doesn't sound like the proper behavior of a Buddha, but Shakyamuni's intention was to awaken Devadatta to the seriousness of his transgression as well as to alert others to avoid similar behavior.

President Ikeda explains Shakyamuni's criticism of Devadatta: "Shakyamuni thoroughly reproached Devadatta's evil. There is no doubt about that. It is by denouncing evil that we can cause such people to open their eyes. That is because hearing voices resounding with the justice of the Mystic Law has the effect of activating the Buddha nature that lies dormant in an evil person's heart. But because such a person's heart is covered with a thick, rocklike crust of ignorance, a weak voice will not reach it. It takes a voice of censure, one that strictly takes evil to task, to break through this hard crust and illuminate the Buddha nature" (June 2003 *Living Buddhism*, pp. 37–38).

It is only when Shakyamuni defeated Devadatta that he could reveal the function of his enemy as a "good friend" born together with him in lifetime after lifetime. In the "Devadatta" (twelfth) chapter of the Lotus Sutra, Shakyamuni reveals that in some past existence he himself had learned the Lotus Sutra from a seer named Asita, and that this seer was Devadatta. He also predicts that Devadatta will attain enlightenment in the future as a Buddha named Heavenly King. Nichiren uses this prediction to illustrate the principle that even evil persons have the potential for enlightenment.

Identify the arrogance of those who pretend to be sages.

In more recent times, this scenario has been played out in the Soka Gakkai's efforts to widely propagate the Law during its association with the Nichiren Shoshu priesthood. In 1990, the behavior of the high priest, Nikken, mirrored the Buddhist definitions of devilish functions explained in the Lotus Sutra as a modern-day Devadatta. The Chinese teacher Miao-lo (711–782) defines these functions on the basis of descriptions in the "Encouraging Devotion" (thirteenth) chapter of the Lotus Sutra. The third powerful enemy is identified by "the arrogance and presumption of those who pretend to be sages" — in other words, arrogant false sages. "This third category is described as priests who pretend to be sages and who are revered as such, but when encountering the practitioners of the Lotus Sutra become fearful of losing fame or profit and induce secular authorities to persecute them" (*The Soka Gakkai Dictionary of Buddhism*, p. 720).

The Nichiren Shoshu priesthood initiated a plan to take control of the SGI laity and remove President Ikeda as the leader of the Buddhist lay community. They issued an order to disband the Soka Gakkai and demanded belief in an infallible high priest, who somehow infused the Gohonzon with power. They claimed to be a clergy to which practitioners must defer for a proper connection to the Daishonin's teachings. In a final, futile, display of authoritarian behavior, Nikken excommunicated the 10 million SGI members around the world. Attempting to destroy the organization that is accomplishing worldwide propagation of the Daishonin's Buddhism falls into the category of evil behavior.

When discussing good and evil behavior, it is important to

> ■ The third powerful enemy is identified by the arrogance and presumption of those who pretend to be sages—in other words, arrogant false sages. This third category includes priests who claim to understand Nichiren Daishonin's teachings, but become fearful of losing fame or profit and induce secular authorities to persecute those who embrace Nichiren's true intent.

> ■ It is in the spirit of Shakyamuni admonishing Devadatta that the SGI is critical of the Nichiren Shoshu priesthood. We must not confuse challenging distortions of the teachings we embrace as intolerance. To ignore the spread of mistaken teachings is not tolerance; it is irresponsible.

provide the correct context. Inflammatory language out of context of the Buddhist life-philosophy can appear to be punitive or hateful. It is not. Our struggle is against the fundamental darkness that exists in all life.

When we see evil in others, we see the potential for evil within ourselves as well. By speaking out against any action that hinders the propagation of the Law, we strengthen our power to contain the evil within us. It should be with this understanding that we apply Buddhist principles and terms concerning evil, because the language we use can confuse rather than educate, polarize rather than unite.

It is crucial that we address evil or devilish functions in the course of our practice and our efforts for *kosen-rufu*. To be passive in the face of such forces would be self-defeating, because these forces themselves are not passive. Nichiren states, "To hope to attain Buddhahood without speaking out against slander is as futile as trying to find water in the midst of fire or fire in the midst of water" (WND-1, 747).

It is in the spirit of Shakyamuni admonishing Devadatta that the SGI is critical of the Nichiren Shoshu priesthood. We must not confuse challenging distortions of the teachings we embrace as intolerance. To ignore the spread of mistaken teachings is not tolerance; it is irresponsible. Tolerance is only credible when it is also clear what is intolerable. We cannot tolerate teachings that diminish the value of human life and inhibit a practitioner's ability to overcome suffering. To simply say we tolerate everything is to imply that we have no beliefs and no principles.

Geography of the Heart

The priesthood upholds the view that, without venerating the high priest, practitioners cannot attain enlightenment—a view that undermines the self-empowering properties of Nichiren Buddhism and the mentor-disciple relationship traditionally taught in all Buddhism. This is a relationship of oneness that results when self-reliant disciples voluntarily choose to take responsibility for the same goal of *kosen-rufu* as their mentor.

The priesthood asserts that the high priest of Nichiren Shoshu, and only he, has the power to determine who attains Buddhahood and who does not: "The master gives his sanction to a disciple's enlightenment.... The sanctioning of the object of worship by the High Priest, who is the only person to be bequeathed the Daishonin's Buddhism, is what makes the attainment of Buddhahood possible..."(*Refuting the Soka Gakkai's "Counterfeit Object of Worship": 100 Questions and Answers* [West Hollywood: Nichiren Shoshu Temple, 1996], p. 8).

> ■ Dr. Bryan Wilson, of Oxford University: "What emerges from the reactions of the priesthood to this openness to international cultures [of the Soka Gakkai] is the narrow parochialism which prevails within this closed religious caste, cut off from the currents of contemporary thought, and interpreting their spiritual inheritance as a limited and localized experience....

"(Believers should have) single-minded faith in him [the high priest] as the living body of Shakyamuni (Nichiren)" (September 2008 *Nichiren Shoshu Monthly*, p. 22).

"The place where the Heritage of the Law is entrusted to a single person [the high priest] exists in the noble entity that is inseparable with the Dai-Gohonzon" (October 2008 *Nichiren Shoshu Monthly*, p. 17).

Rather than recognizing the intent this Gohonzon embodies for the enlightenment of all humanity, however, the priests interpret their possession of it as giving them, and specifically the high priest, exclusive authority and power over all believers. They believe the high

■ "Without these endeavors by Soka Gakkai, Nichiren Shoshu would have remained an obscure Japanese sect, unknown to the outside world, and perhaps of little significance even within Japan. In affirming Buddhism as a life-affirming religion, Soka Gakkai has rescued Japanese Buddhism from its preoccupations with funeral rites for the dead.

Evelyn McGeever/Stockphoto

priest has the power to "turn on" or "turn off" benefit for any believer.

In 1991, as an expression of personal animosity, he pronounced that by removing his sanction the high priest had "turned off" the benefit of all members of the Soka Gakkai and SGI. In the years since, however, millions upon millions of members have clearly and indisputably disproved this childish and ridiculous contention.

While the priesthood claims its physical possession of the Dai-Gohonzon at its head temple automatically affords it mysterious powers and authority, the SGI views the Dai-Gohonzon in accord with Nichiren Daishonin's true intent. Nichiren Daishonin inscribed his immense compassion for all humankind in the Gohonzon.

He never intended that any Gohonzon should give one person or group exclusive powers or authority over others. Nor did he teach anywhere in his writings that people must physically pray before a specific Gohonzon, such as the Dai-Gohonzon, in addition to the one enshrined in their homes, to achieve benefit. Nor did he teach anywhere that one must visit a specific location in Japan or anywhere else to achieve enlightenment.

What he did say was, "Never seek this Gohonzon outside yourself" (WND-1, 832), and "Shakyamuni ... the Lotus Sutra ... and we ordinary human beings are in no way different or separate from one another" (WND-1, 216).

In *The Record of the Orally Transmitted Teachings*, Nichiren succinctly makes this point: "The place where the person upholds and honors the Lotus Sutra is the 'place of practice' to which the person proceeds. It is not that he leaves his present place and goes to some other place. The 'place of practice' is the place where the living beings of the Ten Worlds reside. And now the place where Nichiren and his followers chant Nam-myoho-renge-kyo, 'whether... in mountain valleys or the wide wilderness' (chapter twenty-one, Supernatural Powers), these places are all the Land of Eternally Tranquil Light" (p. 192).

No place is in and of itself a Buddha land; a place becomes a Buddha land when the people there reveal their innate Buddhahood through their faith and practice. It is not that people become Buddhas because they visit a Buddha land; rather, they make the place where they are a Buddha land when they bring forth their Buddha nature.

It is also ironic that the priesthood places such importance on making a pilgrimage to Taiseki-ji, its head temple, when this was a practice initiated by second Soka Gakkai president Toda in 1952. Nichiren Shoshu temples sustained significant damage during World War II. Much of the head temple burned down, and many branch temples were destroyed in air raids. Furthermore, in December 1945, Taiseki-ji lost much of its land in the postwar agrarian reform.

In November 1950, the priesthood held a conference at the reception hall to discuss plans to promote Taiseki-ji as a tourist attraction to generate additional income. Conference participants proposed a scenic road, a tourist information center and a new lodging facility.

Hearing of this plan to turn the head temple into a tourist attraction, President Toda was enraged. His strong opposition prevented the plan from being realized. Instead, to relieve the head temple of its financial burden, Mr. Toda organized group pilgrimages by Soka Gakkai members to Taiseki-ji. This practice continued until Nikken excommunicated the Soka Gakkai and the SGI in 1991

> ■ "It is by diffusion of commitment and its manifestation in the everyday life and service of believers that a religion develops its influence and fulfills its mission. The particularistic devotion to a place— significant as it may be in the formative period of religious development—must give place to a universalistic spirit if that religion is to become a major influence in world affairs.
> *Daibyakurenge* (the Soka Gakkai monthly study journal), January 1992."

Seikyo Press

The priesthood is focused on the geography of the land; the SGI is focused on the geography of the heart—"It is the heart that is important" (WND-1, 951). Nowhere does Nichiren say that physically visiting a specific religious site is important. His statement that the "heart is important" specifically means that faith—in this case the sincerity of the lay nun Sennichi, who could not come to see him—is more important than physical proximity.

Most of what we know of Nichiren's views on the Gohonzon was written prior to October 12, 1279, the date attributed to the inscription of the Dai-Gohonzon. In 1272, he wrote to Abutsu-bo: "Abutsu-bo is therefore the treasure tower itself, and the treasure tower is Abutsu-bo himself.... Faith like yours is so extremely rare that I will inscribe the treasure tower especially for you. You must never transfer it to anyone but your son. You must never show it to others unless they have steadfast faith. This is the reason for my advent in this world" (WND-1, 299¬300). In 1273, he wrote: "I, Nichiren, have inscribed my life in sumi ink, so believe in the Gohonzon with your whole heart" (WND-1, 412). And in 1277 he wrote: "How wondrous it is that, around two hundred years and more into the Latter Day of the Law, I was the first to reveal as the banner of propagation of the Lotus Sutra this great mandala" (WND-1, 831).

The Banner of Propagation

That Nichiren went from words of caution concerning the Gohonzon in 1272 to proclaiming it to be "the banner of propagation" in 1277 can be attributed to the strength of faith his followers developed during that period. Soon after his exile to Sado Island in 1271, he realized that most of the believers in the capital of Kamakura had

quit their faith because they were confused by his continued persecution. He addressed their doubts in his treatise "The Opening of the Eyes." After his pardon from exile and return to the mainland, government persecution was directed at his followers—in particular, the believers in Atsuhara where propagation activities were led by Nichiren's immediate successor, Nikko Shonin. When faced with the full weight of government authority, including incarceration and execution, the farmer-believers did not waiver.

SGI President Ikeda states: "The followers in Atsuhara were neither nobles nor samurai nor priests; they were farmers occupying a low status in society. Yet these nameless practitioners of the Mystic Law did not retreat a single step in the face of persecution by corrupt priests and highhanded samurai officials misusing their authority. No one, no matter how powerful, could make them give up their faith. This was a struggle for human rights that shines with jewel-like brilliance in the history of the ordinary people of Japan" (*The World of Nichiren Daishonin's Writings*, vol. 1, p. 179). Nichiren viewed the appearance of ordinary people who were willing to struggle with the same spirit as him as proof that the Gohonzon should be widely propagated.

■ Yet these nameless practitioners of the Mystic Law did not retreat a single step in the face of persecution by corrupt priests and highhanded samurai officials misusing their authority. No one, no matter how powerful, could make them give up their faith.

This mandate to widely propagate the teaching of chanting Nam-myoho-renge-kyo to the Gohonzon is the purpose of the Dai-Gohonzon's inscription. The idea set forth by the priesthood that practitioners must chant to a particular Gohonzon—that the priesthood owns—to gain the ultimate benefit is an obvious attempt to manipulate temple members and flies in the face of the Daishonin's admonition, "Never seek this Gohonzon outside yourself.... This Gohonzon also is found only in the two characters for faith.... What is most important is that, by chanting Nam-myoho-renge-kyo alone, you can attain Buddhahood. It will no doubt

depend on the strength of your faith. To have faith is the basis of Buddhism" (WND-1, 832). The priesthood's emphasis on what is external over what is internal is contrary to the heart of Nichiren Buddhism.

The SGI view that the power of the Dai-Gohonzon is not contained in a material object but resides in the faith of believers is a teaching of Nichiren's that has been embraced by the Soka Gakkai since its inception. Second Soka Gakkai president Toda said: "While we may think that we are praying to the Dai-Gohonzon outside us, when we chant Nam-myoho-renge-kyo believing in the Gohonzon of the Three Great Secret Laws, the Dai-Gohonzon in fact dwells within our own life. This is a most wondrous teaching" (*Collected Writings of Josei Toda*, vol. 6, p. 608).

This is the time for the worldwide propagation of the Daishonin's ultimate teaching—the Gohonzon. This is the Buddha's will, and it is not limited to a few acres of land in Japan or a single mandala. The Gohonzon and the practice of Nichiren Buddhism can relieve the suffering of all humanity. To distort the teachings with formalities, rituals and falsehoods to promote the personal agenda of the priesthood is a clear example of the devilish nature of life depicted in Buddhist scriptures.

The priesthood's contention that one must visit the Nichiren Shoshu head temple and Japan and physically pray to the Gohonzon enshrined there to attain enlightenment has absolutely no basis in Nichiren Daishonin's teachings. It is designed solely to gain revenue and to make believers dependent on a priesthood that has chosen a course of obstructing and slandering those who practice Nichiren's teachings with the correct spirit. As such, allowing ourselves to be fooled by them and visiting Taiseki-ji amounts to complicity in their slander, a cause that will erase rather than enhance our good fortune.

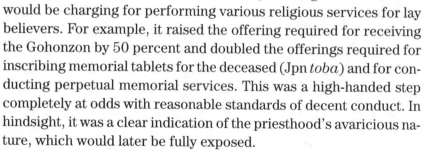

In these excerpts from his Nov. 25, 2003, speech, SGI President Ikeda addresses the actions of Nichiren Shoshu priests surrounding the split with the SGI now celebrated as an event of spiritual independence. The complete text appears in the Feb. 27, 2004, issue of the World Tribune.

The People Are Sovereign
SGI President Ikeda's Speech

As I mentioned at the recent Soka Gakkai Headquarters Leaders Meeting [on Nov. 13, 2003], this month it has been twelve years since the Nichiren Shoshu priesthood sent the Soka Gakkai its Notice of Excommunication [dated Nov. 28, 1991]. We have many new youth now, and for their sake please allow me to once again relate the unfolding of events at that time.

In March 1990, the priesthood, without any discussion with the Soka Gakkai, arbitrarily announced that it was increasing the amounts of monetary offering it would be charging for performing various religious services for lay believers. For example, it raised the offering required for receiving the Gohonzon by 50 percent and doubled the offerings required for inscribing memorial tablets for the deceased (Jpn *toba*) and for conducting perpetual memorial services. This was a high-handed step completely at odds with reasonable standards of decent conduct. In hindsight, it was a clear indication of the priesthood's avaricious nature, which would later be fully exposed.

In April 1990, the No. 2 General Lodging Temple (a lodging for pilgrimage participants) was completed at the head temple under my sponsorship. (The No. 1 General Lodging Temple had been completed in 1988.) In 1990 alone, in addition to this second lodging temple, the Soka Gakkai had built eight branch temples for the priesthood at various locations around Japan. Incidentally, in total, the Soka Gakkai has built 356 temples, 320 of which were built while I was president.

> ■ In the early 1990s, the priesthood started to carry out duplicitous plans to disband the SGI.

Also, over the years, we conducted countless group pilgrimages to the head temple—the aggregate attendance coming to more than 70 million—and we made concerted efforts to enhance the facilities at Taiseki-ji, including sponsoring the construction of the Grand Main Temple (Sho-Hondo) and the Grand Reception Hall (Daikyakuden).

In the land reforms carried out after World War II, the grounds of Taiseki-ji were drastically reduced to less than 42 acres. Through the Soka Gakkai's contributions over the years, however, the head temple grounds now encompass more than 816 acres, a size unprecedented in the temple's history.

Because of our generous support of the priesthood, successive high priests Nissho, Nichijun and Nittatsu [the 64th high priest, Nissho; the 65th high priest, Nichijun; and the 66th high priest, Nittatsu] expressed deep appreciation and praise for the Soka Gakkai.

In particular, 1990 marked the 700th anniversary of Taiseki-ji's founding, and to celebrate that occasion, the local Shizuoka youth conducted a wonderful culture festival in September. Yet, while the youth worked so hard on preparations for that event, High Priest Nikken and his cronies were meeting at Taiseki-ji's Tokyo Office in Nishikata, Bunkyo Ward (on July 16), and at a lecture hall on the head temple grounds (on July 18), hatching a plot to destroy the Soka Gakkai, which they called Operation C ["C" standing for "cut"].

This is just the kind of intrigue aimed at obstructing *kosen-rufu* that the Daishonin refers to when he writes: "People hate me and ceaselessly plot in secret to do me injury" (WND-1, 330). "Evil and unworthy actions such as these on the part of Gyochi continued to pile up day after day…" (WND-2, 827).

During an audience on July 21—just three days after that clandestine

The Grand Main Temple was completed in 1972 through donations of over 8 million Soka Gakkai members and destroyed on orders from High Priest Nikken in 1998.

meeting at the head temple to plot the Soka Gakkai's downfall — High Priest Nikken lashed out at SGI Deputy President Einosuke Akiya, accusing him of slanderous arrogance. Nikken's loss of composure and his overbearing manner were entirely unbefitting the high priest of a Buddhist school.

The Nichiren Shoshu priesthood carried out a duplicitous scheme.

Then, in December, as 1990 was rapidly drawing to a close, the priesthood suddenly sent the Soka Gakkai a letter of inquiry. [This was a document titled "Questions Regarding the Speech of Honorary President Ikeda at the 35th Headquarters Leaders Meeting." This Headquarters Leaders Meeting was held on Nov. 16, 1990, to celebrate the 60th anniversary of the Soka Gakkai.] It contained a list of the most ridiculous charges — such as the accusation that singing Beethoven's great hymn to universal human freedom, "Ode to Joy," constitutes "praise for non-Buddhist teachings." Furthermore, the priesthood demanded a response to their charges within seven days.

Seeking to find out what had prompted this situation, the top Soka Gakkai leadership made every effort to meet and hold a dialogue with head temple representatives, but the priesthood rejected all such requests out of hand.

Then, on Dec. 27, the priesthood convened a special council session, at which they revised the rules of Nichiren Shoshu, thereby dismissing me from the position of head of all Nichiren Shoshu lay organizations and President Akiya and others from the positions of Nichiren Shoshu senior lay representatives. Our members across the nation were stunned by this move. Their New Year's holidays, to which they had been looking forward with such joy and anticipation, were all but ruined. Even now when I think of the pain it caused everyone, my heart aches.

Moreover, in his New Year's message carried in the January 1991 issue of the Soka Gakkai's monthly study journal, the *Daibyakurenge* [which went on sale in mid-December 1990 before these events took place], High Priest Nikken had praised the growth and development of the Soka Gakkai. This was a glaring example of High Priest Nikken being "double-tongued" (WND-1, 324) and "contradicting his own words" (see WND-1, 807), which are regarded as serious offenses in Buddhism. [High Priest Nikken writes in his 1991 New

■ The Daishonin wrote in detail about the nature of arrogant false sages — the third of the three powerful enemies. He described behavior that matches the behavior of Nikken.

Ed Lee

Year's message in the *Daibyakurenge*: "One of the most notable accomplishments of President Ikeda's leadership, in this postwar period of global human migration and exchange, has been the great advance of worldwide *kosen-rufu* through the establishment of local organizations for the members who have appeared in each country. The steady global development of *kosen-rufu* we see today is a wonderful event in the history of Buddhism, in accord with the golden words in 'The Selection of the Time.'"]

At the start of 1991, High Priest Nikken refused to receive Soka Gakkai President Akiya and Soka Gakkai General Director Morita for their customary exchange of New Year's greetings at the head temple, and he shunned meeting with them any time after that as well, stating that they were "unworthy of an audience" with him.

In his writings, the Daishonin describes the cowardly manner in which the infamous Ryokan similarly avoided dialogue: "When I actually did return to Kamakura [from exile on Sado], Ryokan shut his gates and forbade anyone to enter. At times, he even feigned illness, saying that he had caught a cold" (WND-1, 482).

High Priest Nikken, like a modern-day Ryokan, behaved in exactly the same fashion.

Nichiren Daishonin warns of the nature of false sages.

The Daishonin wrote in detail about the nature of arrogant false sages — the third of the three powerful enemies: "They reveal him [Ryokan] very clearly for what he is. First, though by reputation he is an observer of the precepts, in fact he is wanton in conduct. Second, he is greedy and stingy. Third, he is jealous. Fourth, he holds erroneous views. Fifth, he is lewd and disorderly" (WND-2, 693–94).

The Daishonin clearly exposes Ryokan's true nature. High Priest Nikken is also the epitome of a false sage.

Ryokan persecuted the Daishonin and his followers with every means he could summon. In the same way, High Priest Nikken sought to persecute and cut off the Soka Gakkai.

Allow me to return to the subject of the letter of inquiry sent by the priesthood. Since the priesthood continued to reject our request for dialogue on the matter, we eventually sent a written response in which we protested their unfounded accusations and pointed out the inaccuracies in their transcription of the speech deriving from a tape of questionable origin.

As a result, the priesthood was forced to acknowledge several errors in their transcript, and they retracted the questions related to those fallacious quotations. Their retraction destroyed the entire foundation for their spurious contentions. But instead of issuing an official apology, they then tried to stir up trouble in our SGI organizations overseas and to intimidate and alarm everyone through various means, such as refusing to confer Gohonzon on Soka Gakkai members.

> ■ All of the aberrations of Nichiren Shoshu have been laid bare for the world to see: the plot to try to destroy the movement for *kosen-rufu*, the false creed of worshiping the high priest, the erroneous view of the true heritage of Law, the misuse of priestly ceremonies and services, the discrimination that places priests above the laity, and the general corruption and degeneration that pervades the school.

The banning of our members from the head temple is our medal of honor.

The Daishonin, referring to the Lotus Sutra teaching that "evil demons will take possession of others," writes: "He [the devil king of the sixth heaven] possesses...foolish priests such as Ryokan, and causes them to hate me" (WND-1, 310).

Numerous events demonstrate that beneath the plot to disrupt the harmonious unity of the believers lies High Priest Nikken's collusion with what Buddhism terms an *evil companion* — an individual whom High Priest Nikken himself once denounced as resembling Devadatta

[Shakyamuni's archenemy].

The Daishonin writes: "[In this way] did evil persons throw in their lot with Devadatta" (WND-1, 147). "Devadatta kept watch on the Buddha's activities and with a large stone caused his [the Buddha's] blood to flow" (WND-1, 146).

In other words, it is as if a modern-day Devadatta and Ryokan joined forces to destroy the Soka Gakkai, an organization faithfully carrying out the Buddha's intent and decree.

The priesthood then sent us a notice announcing that the existing Soka Gakkai-operated monthly pilgrimage system would be abolished. Under a new system to be implemented directly under the priesthood's control, Soka Gakkai members would now have to register with their local temples to obtain the necessary documents permitting them to visit Taiseki-ji. In other words, the priesthood attempted to use pilgrimages as a means to manipulate our members into submission. Their efforts were in vain, however, because our members refused to be taken in or swayed by such tactics.

When the Japanese militarist authorities arrested the first and second Soka Gakkai presidents, Tsunesaburo Makiguchi and Josei Toda, during World War II, the priesthood callously prohibited them and all Soka Gakkai members from visiting Taiseki-ji and any other Nichiren Shoshu branch temple.

Similarly, in 1952, when a group of youth launched their so-called Operation Tanuki Festival, confronting a slanderous priest over his traitorous actions during the war, the Nichiren Shoshu Council convened to dismiss President Toda as Nichiren Shoshu senior lay representative and ban him from visiting the head temple.

President Toda wrote about that latter decision in his "Epigrams" column in the *Seikyo Shimbun* at the time: "I thought I'd receive a reward for my loyalty in rebuking slander of the Law, but instead of praise, they handed me a reproof: 'You're banned from visiting the

■ President Toda declared: "To betray the Soka Gakkai is to betray the Daishonin. You'll know what I mean when you see the retribution they incur at the end of their lives."

Seikyo Press

head temple!' My disciples replied in unison, 'Then we won't visit either, so there!'"

"When they asked me, I smiled and said: 'Don't make such a fuss. It's a cause for celebration.'

"As described in the Lotus Sutra, one of the tricks of the three kinds of evildoers is to banish the sutra's votaries 'to a place far removed from towers and temples.'"

"Now the Buddha has bestowed upon me the distinguished medal of honor of being banished 'from towers and temples' as proof that I am a great leader of propagation."

"I smiled and asked, 'Are the members of the Nichiren Shoshu Council the second or third of the three powerful enemies?'"

Just as President Toda wisely understood, the banning of Gakkai pilgrimages to the head temple could also indeed be described as a medal of honor from the Daishonin.

■ President Makiguchi said, "The harder we fight and the stronger we become, the more swiftly actual proof of victory in our Buddhist practice appears."

Seikyo Press

The Soka Gakkai conducted and oversaw the running of group pilgrimages to Taiseki-ji with the greatest care and attention to detail, praying constantly that such visits would take place safely, without accidents. Through these painstaking efforts, we established the brilliant record of welcoming more than 70 million visitors to the head temple [over a 40-year period].

It is quite possible, however, that had our pilgrimages continued at that pace, a major accident may have occurred.

The Daishonin was always deeply concerned about his disciples' safety. With this thought foremost in mind, he urged Shijo Kingo to refrain from visiting him at Minobu as long as the journey there and back remained dangerous.

How immeasurably profound in every sense the Buddha wisdom and the Daishonin's consideration have proven to be.

I am sure that those of you who worked so hard to organize those visits to the head temple and ensure the members' safety will appreciate this ever more deeply as the years go by.

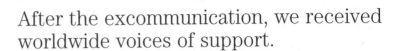

After the excommunication, we received worldwide voices of support.

In November 1991, in what were blatant attempts at intimidation, the priesthood sent the Soka Gakkai an order to disband (dated Nov. 7) and then a notice of excommunication (dated Nov. 28). Unfazed, however, our members joyfully celebrated the day of our excommunication as signaling our spiritual independence from the corrupt priesthood.

On Dec. 27, a month later — a year after the priesthood dismissed me as head of all Nichiren Shoshu lay organizations — the Soka Gakkai sent a petition demanding High Priest Nikken's resignation from the position of high priest. Some 16.25 million people worldwide signed our petition. So it turns out it was High Priest Nikken instead who had been "excommunicated" by a global alliance of Bodhisattvas of the Earth, 16.25 million strong.

At the same time, upright priests of good conscience took a stand and announced their solidarity with us as comrades in faith dedicated to *kosen-rufu*. All told, thirty temples and fifty-three priests left Nichiren Shoshu.

Thoughtful and informed people around the globe also began to speak out in great numbers to support and defend the Soka Gakkai. Today, with gratitude to each of them, allow me to share a few of those statements with you.

Professor Nur Yalman of Harvard University is a renowned cultural anthropologist. Following my second Harvard address in September 1993, Professor Yalman told an audience of distinguished educators and scholars that just as the

Protestant Reformation had been a landmark event in the history of Christianity, the religious reformation being undertaken by the Soka Gakkai was a development of great significance in the history of Buddhism. The Soka Gakkai's remarkable reform movement, he noted, would have important implications not only for Buddhism but other religious traditions as well. He described it as representing a new departure and a new development in the history of religion.

> ■ Let us also never relax in our struggle, fighting on for justice to the very end, just as the Daishonin teaches.

Dr. David Norton, an eminent professor of philosophy at the University of Delaware, voiced his powerful conviction [in 1991], saying: "The priesthood, in its attack on the activities of the Soka Gakkai which has been extending a network of peace and culture throughout Japan and the world, is guilty of what can only be described as profound myopia, or even blindness. If asked the cause of that blindness, I'm afraid my only response would be, 'Jealousy.'" He further said, "The priesthood's notice of excommunication goes completely against Nichiren's teaching that all people possess the Buddha nature and that this precious potential must never be closed off or denied."

Great minds outside Japan clearly see the outrageous and foolhardy actions of the priesthood in their true light.

A progressive lay movement stands in contrast to an anachronistic priesthood.

Shin Anzai, professor emeritus of Japan's Sophia University and a leading Japanese sociologist of religion, offered his views as follows: "In recent years the Soka Gakkai has begun to walk a new path as a lay religious organization separate from the priesthood. I view this as an inevitable result of the fundamental difference between the open, progressive Soka Gakkai and the closed, conservative priesthood. The priesthood has become an anachronism, showing no understanding of the value of peace, culture, and education, clinging to hidebound traditions and attempting to control lay followers by authority and force. Had the Soka Gakkai not claimed its independence from the priesthood, it would have eventually been fated to become a self-righteous and closed religious organization, too, its bright future and global development perishing. Japanese intellectuals and journalists need to know this fact, but they completely fail to understand it. I believe this arises from a kind of envy [toward the Soka Gakkai] — the same problem that afflicts the priesthood."

Tetsuro Aramaki, professor emeritus of Kanazawa Seiryo University (formerly Kanazawa University of Economics) and respected economist, observed: "The priesthood, which by rights should be dedicated to the salvation of all living beings, in its demands that the lay body Soka Gakkai disband, shows a callousness totally inappropriate for a religious organization."

In addition, Yukio Kamono of Asahi University, a noted law professor who is also a professor emeritus of Kanazawa University, said: "When I heard about the Notice of Excommunication, in general I must say that I felt it was an arbitrary and extreme measure. To excommunicate an entire organization without any discussion, just a single sheet of paper — from the perspective of normal legal procedure as well — is highly irregular."

And Professor Kuniyasu Take of Kyoto's Doshisha Women's College of Liberal Arts argued: "Why is the priesthood seeking to disband an organization of its lay believers [the Soka Gakkai], which is dedicated to the spiritual liberation of people around the world? I feel compelled to point out the suicidal behavior of the priesthood."

The courageous statements of these learned figures are certain to shine forever in history.

The emergence of lay leadership is inevitable.

Dr. Bryan Wilson, reader emeritus of Oxford University and the first president of the International Society for the Sociology of Religion, with whom I engaged in a dialogue published as *Human Values in a Changing World: A Dialogue on the Social Role of Religion*, has written on the matter of our 1991 excommunication: "What emerges from the reactions of the priesthood to this openness to international cultures [of the Soka Gakkai] is the narrow parochialism which prevails within this closed religious caste, cut off from the currents of contemporary thought, and interpreting their spiritual inheritance as a limited and localized experience....

"Without these endeavors by Soka Gakkai, Nichiren Shoshu would have remained an obscure Japanese sect, unknown to the outside world, and perhaps of little significance even within Japan. In affirming Buddhism as a life-affirming religion, Soka Gakkai has rescued Japanese Buddhism from its preoccupations with funeral rites for the dead."

Further, Dr. Wilson shared a positive view of the discontinuation of Soka Gakkai pilgrimages to the head temple, noting that "religious faith transcends all such localized symbolism [as represented by Taiseki-ji]." He continued: "It is by diffusion of commitment and its manifestation in the everyday life and service of believers that a religion develops its influence and fulfills its mission. The particularistic devotion to a place — significant as it may be in the formative period of religious development — must give place to a universalistic spirit if that religion is to become a major influence in world affairs."

Dr. Wilson also called the emergence of lay leadership in religion as part of an inevitable historical process, and his assertion has now been borne out beyond a doubt.

To betray the SGI is to betray Nichiren Daishonin.

I have also published a dialogue with the French art historian and champion of the human spirit, René Huyghe, titled *Dawn After Dark*. Mr. Huyghe remarked that the world should thank the Soka Gakkai for promoting the profound values and universality of Buddhism, as well as for its efforts to advance world peace by elevating the human spirit based on Buddhist ideals.

Anyone, he said, would surely lament disreputable attacks motivated by hunger for power or material gain that might hinder the Soka Gakkai's admirable efforts to uplift humanity and its splendid success.

Dr. Howard Hunter, now emeritus professor of religion at Tufts University in the United States, said [in 1991] that he was very interested in observing what kind of effect the excommunication of more than 10 million lay followers by a tiny minority of priests claiming orthodoxy would have on the priests themselves, since it was such an extraordinary thing to do. He added that when a religious group loses touch with the hearts of its followers who are striving earnestly to apply their religious beliefs in society and the real world, that group is on the road to ossification.

Twelve years have passed since we received the Notice of Excommunication from the priesthood. As all of you are well aware, our victory in light of Buddhism is crystal clear.

The Daishonin recorded the fate of Ryokan and his colleagues: "You may think that those who believe in Priest Two Fires [Ryokan] are prospering [but this is certainly not the case]" (WND-1, 638). The strict retribution befalling High Priest Nikken and his cohorts is proof that they have been excommunicated and condemned by the Daishonin himself.

Today, all of the aberrations of Nichiren Shoshu have been laid bare for the world to see: the plot to try to destroy the movement for *kosen-rufu*, the false creed of worshiping the high priest, the erroneous view of the true heritage of Law, the misuse of priestly ceremonies and services, the discrimination that places priests above the laity, and the general corruption and degeneration that pervades the school.

In contrast, the Soka Gakkai has become the pillar of Japan and a bright light of hope

for the world. It celebrates its seventy-third anniversary this year with a global network that spans 186 nations and territories [now 192] and with an unprecedented tide of victories.

The Daishonin, the Buddha of the Latter Day of the Law, undoubtedly praises us and smiles on our efforts, while at the same time commanding the protective forces of the universe to keep us safe from harm.

I am equally sure our victory would bring immense delight to President Makiguchi. Our founding president once observed: "How much more serious is the offense of those Buddhist and Shinto priests who stand even further upstream and put poison into the water. In this case, even a small transgression can become an extremely grave offense, making a cause that will bring infinitely evil retribution. How much graver still it is then to oppose great good and contribute to great evil, to bow to great evil and slander great good."

I have always fully agreed with these words. In fact, it is the great evil of High Priest Nikken and his cohorts that resents and envies the great good of the Soka Gakkai.

As champions of the correct teaching, we have resolutely triumphed over the schemes of such malicious forces.

President Makiguchi also said: "The more others slander and despise the Lotus Sutra, the greater the happiness [its votaries will ultimately come to experience as a result of this persecution]. We are certain to win in our struggle. The important thing is to put the principle of 'changing poison into medicine' into practice in our lives."

On another occasion, he said, "The harder we fight and the stronger we become, the more swiftly actual proof of victory in our Buddhist practice appears." We have fought in exact accord with the words of the Soka Gakkai's

Seikyo Press

founder. That is why we have been victorious.

"The final fate of all traitors is a degrading story of suffering and ignominy," said President Makiguchi with keen perception. What he says is absolutely true, as you have seen with your own eyes.

President Toda also declared: "To betray the Soka Gakkai is to betray the Daishonin. You'll know what I mean when you see the retribution they incur at the end of their lives."

And in discussing the Daishonin's "Letter from Sado," he said: "The Daishonin declares that when evil priests ally themselves with evil rulers and persecute those who seek to establish the correct teaching, those who fight against such iniquity with lionhearted courage will surely attain Buddhahood."

President Toda further said: "The Soka Gakkai spirit is to work for the happiness of our country and all countries in the world…. The purpose of *kosen-rufu* is to make it possible for all the world's peoples to live in happiness." And he declared: "Let us be as proud as lion kings! For, according to *The Writings of Nichiren Daishonin*, that is how we will become Buddhas — 'as Nichiren did.'"

The Daishonin admonishes strictly: "Both teacher and followers will surely fall into the hell of incessant suffering if they see enemies of the Lotus Sutra but disregard them and fail to reproach them" (WND-1, 747). "Rather than offering up ten thousand prayers for remedy, it would be better simply to outlaw this one evil" (WND-1, 15). "From now on too, no matter what may happen, you must not slacken in the least. You must raise your voice all the more and admonish [those who slander]" (WND-2, 597).

These are all passages that President Makiguchi and President Toda frequently referred to and cited.

Let us also never relax in our struggle, fighting on for justice to the very end, just as the Daishonin teaches.

Appendix A

Timeline

To explain every event surrounding the separation of the SGI from Nichiren Shoshu is beyond the scope of this booklet. The following timeline highlights most of the important developments. For further explanation, see the references in appendix B.

1989

Feb. 25—Nichiren Shoshu makes a request to the Soka Gakkai to raise the pilgrimage fee.

July 17—Nikken builds a family tomb at a Zen temple, Hakusan-ji in Fukushima, and conducts a commemorative ceremony at the site (breaking one of Nikko Shonin's Twenty-six Admonitions).

1990

March 13—Nichiren Shoshu notifies the Soka Gakkai at a regular communication meeting of an increase in fees for the Gohonzon conferral, toba (memorial tablet) and keeping ashes of the deceased.

July 16—Nikken and some senior priests meet at Taiseki-ji's Tokyo office in Nishikata to discuss how to oust President Ikeda, i.e., how to execute what was later called Operation C. This meeting is later called the Nishikata Conference.

July 17—At the regularly scheduled Nichiren Shoshu and Soka Gakkai communication meeting, the Soka Gakkai raises the issue of unseemly conduct by priests that is becoming rampant throughout Nichiren Shoshu.

July 18—Nikken and the same priests who met at Nishikata meet again to further discuss their plot against President Ikeda. Nikken officially names the plan Operation C. This meeting is later referred to as the Council in the Presence of the High Priest.

July 21—SGI President Ikeda and Soka Gakkai President Akiya are granted an audience with Nikken. During the audience, Nikken emotionally reproaches President Akiya, calling him arrogant. He also attempts to intimidate President Ikeda when he says, "I will impeach you."

Aug. 29—Nichiren Shoshu announces a "Standard of Moral Ethics for Priests and Their Families" at a nationwide meeting of priests.

Sept. 2—The Soka Gakkai dedicates a culture festival to Nichiren Shoshu to celebrate the 700th anniversary of the founding of the head temple, Taiseki-ji.

Oct. 12–13—A grand ceremony to commemorate the 700th anniversary of the founding of Taiseki-ji is held with President Ikeda as the committee chairman.

Nov. 16—President Ikeda gives a speech at the 35th Soka Gakkai Headquarters Leaders Meeting, an unauthorized recording of which Nichiren Shoshu uses to attack him and the Soka Gakkai.

Dec. 13—Nichijun Fujimoto, Nichiren Shoshu general administrator, attempts to hand an inquiry document raising issues concerning the content of the Nov. 16 speech to President Ikeda. Fujimoto withdraws the document when Mr. Akiya requests a dialogue to iron out differences.

Dec. 16— Nichiren Shoshu, refusing to engage in dialogue with the Soka Gakkai, sends the inquiry to the Soka Gakkai Headquarters and demands a written reply.

Dec. 23—The Soka Gakkai responds by sending Nichiren Shoshu a written request for dialogue including questions of its own and concerns about the accuracy of the tape transcription.

Dec. 25—Nikken meets with journalists Isao Dan, Kojun Takahashi and others to discuss attacking the Soka Gakkai in the media.

Dec. 27—Nichiren Shoshu holds a special Council session to revise its rules so it can dismiss President Ikeda from his position as head of all Nichiren Shoshu lay societies, using the tape of his speech as a pretext.

1991

Jan. 1 — The Soka Gakkai points out several errors in the priesthood's transcription of the tape of President Ikeda's speech at the Nov. 16, 1990, Headquarters Leaders Meeting.

Jan. 2 — Nikken refuses to grant an audience to President Akiya and General Director Morita who had requested a meeting to discuss the disagreement.

Jan. 6 — Nikken lectures on the Grand Main Temple, which houses the Dai-Gohonzon, misinterpreting the late high priest Nittatsu's address on the significance of this structure.

Jan. 12 — Nichiren Shoshu, admitting its mistakes in transcribing the tape, withdraws questions at the core of its inquiry. The basis of the priesthood's attacks on the Soka Gakkai and dismissal of President Ikeda thus collapses, but the priesthood makes no move to reverse its decision or discuss reconciliation.

March 5 — Nichiren Shoshu notifies the Soka Gakkai that, henceforth, lay organizations besides the Soka Gakkai can be created overseas, reversing a long-standing policy established during Nittatsu's term. This is the beginning of the priesthood's plan to create temple organizations (*danto*) outside Japan.

March 30 — The Soka Gakkai sends Nikken a second set of questions concerning his misinterpretation of the late high priest Nittatsu's address on the significance of the Grand Main Temple. Nikken does not respond.

July 1 — Nichiren Shoshu abolishes the Soka Gakkai's traditional pilgrimage system of 40 years and starts a new system requiring each participant to have documentation from his or her local temple, thus using access to the Dai-Gohonzon as an enticement aiming to increase the number of direct temple members.

July 21 — At a nationwide meeting of priests, Nikken emphasizes that promoting the direct temple movement (i.e., urging members to leave the SGI and join the temple) is the official direction of Nichiren Shoshu. To make his point, Nikken refers to three things: the revision of the rules of Nichiren Shoshu, the temple's new method of propagating the Daishonin's Buddhism outside Japan and the new pilgrimage system.

Nov. 7 — Nichiren Shoshu sends the Soka Gakkai a document titled "Remonstration to the Soka Gakkai to Disband."

Nov. 28 — Nichiren Shoshu sends the Soka Gakkai a document titled "Notification of the Excommunication of the Soka Gakkai from Nichiren Shoshu," excommunicating more than 12 million believers without any effort to resolve the disagreement through dialogue.

Dec. 27 — The Soka Gakkai sends Nichiren Shoshu a document titled "Seeking the Resignation of Nikken as Nichiren Shoshu High Priest," signed by 16.25 million people.

1992

Feb. 2 — Seven priests, including Reverend Gen'ei Kudo (former chief priest in Los Angeles), leave Nichiren Shoshu, forming the Association of Priests for the Reformation of Nichiren Shoshu.

March 30 — A group of young priests directly confront and question Nikken. With this incident, they leave Nichiren Shoshu and form the Association of Youthful Priests for the Reformation of Nichiren Shoshu.

June 14 — A third group of priests leave Nichiren Shoshu to form the Association Concerned About Nichiren Shoshu and Devoted to Protecting the Law.

June 17 — The *Soka Shimpo*, the Soka Gakkai youth division newspaper, first publishes an article about the Seattle Incident, reporting Mrs. Hiroe Clow's account of Nikken's run-in with prostitutes and police during a Gohonzon-conferral trip to Seattle in 1960 when he was the Nichiren Shoshu Study Department chief.

Aug. 11 — Nichiren Shoshu expels SGI President Ikeda as a lay believer (in effect his second excommunication).

Aug. 28 — At a nationwide meeting of priests, Nikken states that he never set foot outside the hotel in Seattle on the night he is alleged to have had an encounter with prostitutes and police.

1993

April 27 — Masatomo Yamazaki, who was imprisoned for attempting to blackmail the Soka Gakkai, is released on parole. Yamazaki later approaches Nikken and becomes a Hokkeko member belonging to the Rikyo-bo lodging temple at the head temple.

Oct. 2—The Soka Gakkai begins to confer the Gohonzon transcribed by the 26th high priest Nichikan upon its members.

Dec. 4—Nikken goes to Spain to open a Nichiren Shoshu office there.

Dec. 25—Nichiren Shoshu sues the Soka Gakkai in the Tokyo District Court, claiming that the latter's publications' coverage of the Seattle Incident amounts to defamation of Nikken.

1994

Jan. 1—Evidence from within Nichiren Shoshu confirming the existence of Operation C is made public.

June 1—It is revealed that Taiseki-ji has illegally disposed of the ashes of many deceased. A number of lawsuits by individual believers follow, and Nichiren Shoshu loses nearly every case.

July 8—The District Court in Pusan, South Korea, fines Nichiren Shoshu priest Hakudo Mori for operating a temple illegally registered as a nursing home.

Aug. 21—At a Hokkeko leaders meeting, Nikken says that he will resign if the Seattle Incident is proven true.

1995

Jan. 20—Priests Chodo Ishibashi and Kan'o Tajima, who were illegally engaged in propagation in Korea, are fined and deported from the country.

Feb. 24—Police investigate the Korean Nichiren Shoshu office.

May 4—Myohon-ji temple in Hota, one of the major time-honored temples, secedes from Nichiren Shoshu.

June-July—The Nichiren Shoshu summer training course pilgrimage is held with fewer than the 50,000-participant goal.

June 6—Chief Abbot of the Nichiren Shu (Minobu sect) Ikegami Homon-ji temple in Tokyo visits Taiseki-ji and is welcomed there — another violation of Nikko Shonin's Twenty-six Admonitions.

Aug. 23—Nichiren Shoshu announces its plan to destroy the Grand Reception Hall.

Aug. 29—Priest Hakudo Mori is fined in Japan for violation of the Foreign

Exchange Control Law in connection with his illegal temple operations in Korea.

Sept. 29—In the Seattle Incident trial, Nikken radically changes his story, acknowledging that he did leave his hotel for a drink the night of the incident.

1996

Sept. 18—Ronald Sprinkle, a former Seattle police officer (who was directly involved in the 1960 Seattle Incident), testifies as a defense witness.

1997

April 18—Seven Nichiren Shoshu priests stationed at the head temple, Taiseki-ji, participate in the *omushibarai* ceremony at the Honmon-ji temple of the Minobu sect, another gross violation of Nikko Shonin's Twenty-six Admonitions.

Sept. 17—Thirty Nichiren Shu (Minobu sect) priests visit Taiseki-ji.

Sept. 29—The judge in the Seattle Incident trial decides that Nikken must testify, despite his attorneys' protests. Nichiren Shoshu changes its rules again, making it easier to expel believers.

Oct. 6—Nikken abruptly fires his chief attorney.

Nov. 30—Nichiren Shoshu excommunicates all Soka Gakkai members a second time (the third time for President Ikeda).

Dec. 22—Nikken appears in court and presents his never-before-revealed diary that he alleges to have used at the time of the Seattle Incident. It indicates that he was back in his hotel room by the time of the alleged incident. Later, the defense shows that these diary entries had been altered.

1998

Feb. 2—Attorneys for the Soka Gakkai question Nikken in the Seattle Incident trial.

March 26—Another major Nichiren Shoshu pilgrimage is held, but again the goal of 100,000 participants is not met. The new Grand Reception Hall is opened. Nikken destroyed the one built by the Soka Gakkai.

April 5—Nikken secretly transfers the Dai-Gohonzon from the Grand Main Temple to the Hoanden.

May 14—A Brazilian court enforces its decision to oust Nichiren Shoshu priests who had illegally occupied the main part of Ichijo-ji temple.

May 18—Attorneys for the Soka Gakkai question Nikken a second time in the Seattle Incident trial.

June 23—Nikken begins demolition of the Grand Main Temple.

July 2—Argentina's Bureau of Religion bans Nichiren Shoshu as a religious corporation after a priest stationed there, in a sermon and in print, calls Mother Teresa a devil.

1999

January—Nichijun Fujimoto, Nichiren Shoshu general administrator, and Shinsho Abe, Nikken's son and vice chief of the General Affairs Bureau, tour Japan (through March 31) to put pressure on local priests who are not showing good results in terms of membership participation and donations.

Feb. 20—Nichiren Shoshu discloses its plan to collect from its members $50 million per year for the next three years toward 2002.

April 29—Ho'on-ji temple in Chiba secedes from Nichiren Shoshu.

July 7—The "Kawabe Memo" becomes public. It records Nikken's past statements indicating his belief that the Dai-Gohonzon is a forgery.

Aug. 20—Zencho-ji temple in Hiroshima secedes from Nichiren Shoshu.

Sept. 9—Daien-ji temple in Kanagawa secedes from Nichiren Shoshu.

2005

March—High Priest Nikken retires and Nichinyo becomes 68th high priest of Nichiren Shoshu. Nikken remains as center of power within the priesthood, and attacks on the Soka Gakkai continue.

Appendix B

Glossary

Fundamental darkness

Also, fundamental ignorance or primal ignorance. The most deeply rooted illusion inherent in life, said to give rise to all other illusions. Darkness in this sense means inability to see or recognize the truth, particularly, the true nature of one's life. The term *fundamental darkness* is contrasted with the fundamental nature of enlightenment, which is the Buddha nature inherent in life or enlightenment to the fundamental nature of all things and phenomena.

Kosen-rufu

Wide propagation, or wide proclamation and propagation. A term from the Lotus Sutra that literally means to declare and spread widely. Nichiren (1222–1282), identifying himself as the votary of the Lotus Sutra, made it his lifelong mission to fulfill the above injunction of the Buddha, that is, *kosen-rufu.* He saw widely propagating his teaching of Nam-myoho-renge-kyo, which he identified as the essence of the sutra, as the fulfillment of that mission.

Lotus Sutra

One of the Mahayana sutras. China's T'ien-t'ai (538–597), in *The Profound Meaning of the Lotus Sutra,* formulated a system of classification of the entire body of Buddhist sutras called the "five periods and eight teachings," which ranks the Lotus Sutra above all the other sutras. In Japan, Nichiren (1222–1282) also upheld the Lotus Sutra, which describes all living beings as potential Buddhas, and identified its essence as Nam-myoho-renge-kyo.

Nichiren Shoshu

Literally, "Nichiren Correct school." One of the Nichiren schools, whose head temple is Taiseki-ji in Shizuoka Prefecture, Japan. This school regards Nichiren as the Buddha of the Latter Day of the Law and recognizes his teaching of "sowing" implicit in the "Life Span" (sixteenth) chapter of the Lotus Sutra. In 1930 the Soka Kyoiku Gakkai (Value-Creating Education Society) was inaugurated by Tsunesaburo Makiguchi (1871–1944) and Josei Toda (1900–1958), who had converted to Nichiren Shoshu. From the early 1930s through the Second World War, imperial Japan tried to unify the people with State Shinto as the spiritual backbone of wars it fought and the Peace Preservation Law of 1925 as the means for thought control. Under this system, the Nichiren Shoshu priesthood complied with the militarist government's command of Shinto worship, which Makiguchi refused despite the urging of the priesthood. As a result, charged with violation of the Peace Preservation Law and with lese majesty against the emperor and his ancestral god, twenty-one top leaders of the society were arrested and imprisoned. Most of them abandoned their faith and renounced their association with Makiguchi and Toda. Makiguchi upheld his faith and died in prison in 1944. His disciple, Toda, was finally released on parole just before the end of the war and then embarked on the reconstruction of their lay movement, which he renamed Soka Gakkai (Value-Creating Society), and of Nichiren Shoshu, which had been left destitute. In the ensuing years, the Soka Gakkai grew into a substantial worldwide movement with a membership of several million. The priesthood of Nichiren Shoshu, however, found itself ill prepared to deal with an active and socially engaged membership body of this scale. Its 67th chief priest, Nikken, sought to disband the organization and bring its membership directly under his control. The Soka Gakkai resisted this plan and was excommunicated in 1991 by Nikken. Contrary to Nikken's plans, however, the Soka Gakkai

continued to grow and flourish after the excommunication. Nichiren Shoshu maintained a posture of appealing to Soka Gakkai members to leave the organization and directly believe in and support the Nichiren Shoshu priesthood. To do so, they promulgated a doctrine ascribing to their chief priest certain unique and special powers and implied that he alone was the living equivalent of Nichiren. The Soka Gakkai held that this doctrine had nothing to do with the teachings of Nichiren, the spiritual founder of both groups, and thus constituted a misrepresentation of his teachings.

Three obstacles and four devils

Various obstacles and hindrances to the practice of Buddhism. The three obstacles are (1) the obstacle of earthly desires, or obstacles arising from the three poisons of greed, anger, and foolishness; (2) the obstacle of karma, obstacles due to bad karma created by committing any of the five cardinal sins or ten evil acts; and (3) the obstacle of retribution, obstacles caused by the negative karmic effects of actions in the three evil paths. In a letter he addressed to the Ikegami brothers in 1275, Nichiren states, "The obstacle of earthly desires is the impediments to one's practice that arise from greed, anger, foolishness, and the like; the obstacle of karma is the hindrances presented by one's wife or children; and the obstacle of retribution is the hindrances caused by one's sovereign or parents" (WND, 501). The four devils are (1) the hindrance of the five components, obstructions caused by one's physical and mental functions; (2) the hindrance of earthly desires, obstructions arising from the three poisons; (3) the hindrance of death, meaning one's own untimely death obstructing one's practice of Buddhism, or the premature death of another practitioner causing one to doubt; and (4) the hindrance of the devil king, who is said to assume various forms or take possession of others in order to cause one to discard one's Buddhist practice. This hindrance is regarded as the most difficult to overcome.

Three powerful enemies

Three types of arrogant people who persecute those who propagate the Lotus Sutra in the evil age after Shakyamuni Buddha's death. (1) "The arrogance and presumption of lay people" or arrogant lay people; a reference to those ignorant of Buddhism who curse and speak ill of the practitioners of the Lotus Sutra and attack them with swords and staves. (2) "The arrogance and presumption of members of the Buddhist clergy" or arrogant priests. These are priests with perverse wisdom and hearts that are fawning and crooked who, though failing to understand Buddhism, boast they have attained the Buddhist truth and slander the sutra's practitioners. (3) "The arrogance and presumption of those who pretend to be sages" or arrogant false sages. This third category is described as priests who pretend to be sages and who are revered as such, but when encountering the practitioners of the Lotus Sutra become fearful of losing fame or profit and induce secular authorities to persecute them. In On "The Words and Phrases," Miao-lo sates, "Of these three, the first can be endured. The second exceeds the first, and the third is the most formidable of all. This is because the second and third ones are increasingly harder to recognize for what they really are." Nichiren (1222–1282) called them the "three powerful enemies" and identified himself as the votary, or true practitioner, of the Lotus Sutra because he was subjected to slander, attacked with swords and staves, and sent into exile twice by the authorities, just as prophesied in the sutra.

Source: *The Soka Gakkai Dictionary of Buddhism*

Appendix C

For More Information

The history and concepts relating to Soka Spirit are explored in *The Untold History of the Fuji School* and *Buddhism In a New Light*.

For a deeper understanding of the Buddhist principles covered in this pamphlet, read *The Wisdom of the Lotus Sutra*, vols. 1–6, and *The World of Nichiren Daishonin's Writings*, vols. 1–4. These books and more are available at SGI-USA bookstores or our online bookstore at www.sgi-usa.org (then click on "SGI-USA Online Store").

Also, visit the Soka Spirit Website at www.sokaspirit.org and check out the archives and free downloads.